How To
LOVE
The Clients You Really Want
TO HATE

A Melting Pot Of Personalities That Can
Make Or Break Your Business

Trish Rock

ISBN: 13-978-1470053710

ISBN: 10-1470053713

'*Our life is a journey of discovery that involves all of us as a whole.*

Embrace and appreciate all who come into your life as they are there to serve you and show you the way to your inner peace, love and truth.'

Trish Rock

Dedication

This book is dedicated to all of the clients that have made my life what it is today. The good, the bad and the in between- you have all played a part in my experience, as I have in yours, and I am grateful.

Without you, not only would my businesses have been nonexistent, but my life would have been far less than it is today.

I would also like to thank the Entrepreneurs of the world, and in my world, for the inspiration to write this book and it is with much gratitude I put pen to paper in the anticipation that these words will assist you in your every day dealings with clients.

My wish for you, the reader, is that you will gain insight and strength from the words presented in this book and become the person you can be, have the salon you dream of and have the life you deserve.

Trish ☺

PS. All opinions expressed are mine and no harm was done to any clients in the making of this book lol

Contents

How To Love The Clients You Really Want to Hate

A Melting Pot Of Personalities That Will Make Or Break Your Salon

Introduction

> *"When I grow up I want to do peoples nails, hair and makeup.*
>
> *I love to make people look good and feel happy."*

If you have dreamt about being a Nail Technician, Hair Dresser, Makeup artist or Beautician since a young age it is very exciting to see the day arrive when you are qualified and can work in a salon.

After many years of practising on family and friends, to finally have paid clients is not only exciting but a dream come true for many.

For some of us the dream was not a childhood one but still very exciting when the day comes that we have our own business. Take me for instance; I actually studied to be a fashion designer for the last 5 years of my school life. Then when I chose not to follow through with that life path I just 'fell' into the nail business. I embraced it immediately, discovered it was easy for me to do and I loved it for the nearly 30 years I was in it.

The dream of being a salon owner and the actual reality of it can often be a frustrating and testing time. Things will run beautifully for a while as your excitement levels are high and your clients are interesting and new. After a few years you will have a bunch of regular clients that you love and look forward to seeing each month. For some salon owners this will mean the same clients, on the same day at the same time and their books will be more or less closed except for a cancelation list.

Whatever the case may be, as a Nail Technician, Hair Dresser, Makeup Artist or Beautician, we have to deal with many different types of people and personalities on a daily basis.

This type of training is not in the manuals, not in the certificate courses and certainly not in any training schools I have come across lately, or ever.

Naturally I feel if a person has the tendency to go into the salon business they are already a people person. This is a great start but after a while there are different personalities that may be difficult to deal with.

When I thought about putting my thoughts in print for this book, I wondered if it was only me that was annoyed by certain clients.

- Was I just in a bad head space and these clients did not bother other Salon Owners?

- Why did some clients bother me, not others?

- Why did different clients bother me at different stages of my career rather than at others?

While it may be true that the way I was thinking was not always in a good headspace in certain instances, I know for sure that other Nail Technicians, Hair Dressers, Makeup Artists and Beauticians all have to deal with clients they would rather not be dealing with. Whether they are the same ones that bother all of us is hard to say as that will depend on the individual but I am positive that these solutions will help in some way towards having a more flowing salon, free of energy vampires.

I notice a lot of Nail Technicians, Hair Dressers, Makeup Artists and Beauticians reaching out for advice through forums and Social media platforms on how to deal with certain clients and their behaviour so I understand it can be a problem for many people in business, no matter what that business is.

IDEAL CLIENTS

I am a strong believer that of you know who your *ideal clients* are and you market *specifically* for them, the chances of having some of these challenges with clients become a lot less however there will still be the occasions when they do cross your path and you need to know how to deal with them in your salon.

This book will have a look at 5 different types of clients. I will show you first of all why it is that some of these clients do what they do, what has brought them to these habits and how it is a waste of your time and energy to attempt to change them in any way.

My intention is also to show you how all different types of clients can actually help you to grow and become a better, more fulfilled person. When you discover they are in your life to be your teacher, you will see these clients in a totally different light and appreciate them more than ever before.

(This does not mean you have to put up with their behaviour or have them as clients by any means. There are many other clients out there that will value your services.)

Now, that is not to say there will be challenges!

Especially with the notoriously late clients and the no shows but if you can understand them a little better you may not let the situation affect you as it may do now. You may also come to the realisation that when you get frustrated and upset with these clients, you are only hurting yourself because chances are that they don't even know the angst going on inside of you and affecting your health.

The 5 different clients this book will examine are:

- The Late Client
- The Loud/Know It All Client
- The Constant No Show Client
- The Hypochondriac
- The Cheap Client

I will explore how these clients can disrupt the whole routine of your salon, how they can really get under your skin sometimes and I will offer solutions to you for dealing with them.

There may be client profiles covered in this book that do not bother you in particular and you may not understand why they would bother another person. I guess that the way life is with all of us having different personalities we all relate to different people in a different way. Our confidence levels are an important factor in all of this also and as we go along this will be discussed and pointed out as one of the big reasons some clients have the ability to cause us this type of grief in the first place.

Understanding that people don't set out in the morning to deliberately cause disruption to your salon and grief to you plays a big part in the stories I present here for you.

All people have a reason for doing what they do and being who they are so I want to also offer you some possible scenarios that may have been in the lives of these people to have bought them to this place they are in.

Everyone who comes into our lives is there to teach us in some way or another. They may come for a short time or a long period of time, they may be the person who smiles at you in the street or the person whom you love.

When you attract people into your life it is always for a purpose- self growth or expansion.

You may be now asking how on earth a client that continues to be late, not show up or has every ailment under the sun can be of help to you!

We are all here to grow and learn and become more. With the help of all who we come into contact with we can expand and become the person we are meant to be. The road is not always smooth but it is the bumps along the way that give us strength and move us towards our ultimate goals and dreams.

I invite you to enjoy this book, take from it what you need and my wish for you is that you will be at peace with your life and all who come into it.

Once this peace about living in the moment and seeing the blessing in everything and everyobe is present, things will change I can guarantee it.

All of a sudden, those troublesome clients may not be that way any longer, and the days that used to be terribly long and frustrating will soon become an absolute delight full of laughter and happiness.

Enjoy!

Chapter 1

The Late Client

Looking at my appointment schedule this morning as I begin the day I notice that Miss D is coming at 3pm. This could really mess my day up if she is late again! I can't understand why she just cannot get here on time or at least only a few minutes late.

Why does she constantly have to be 10, 15, 20 minutes late or more?

It's infuriating and it messes the whole day up for me! That's it, I'm going to get serious with her today and let her know it's not fair on me or my next clients that we should be held up because of her tardiness!

I am never late and I just don't understand how people cannot look at their watches and get somewhere on time!!

Can you relate to this scenario?

If you have ever experienced clients that are constantly late for their appointments you will totally understand how it messes up your whole day and schedule. Not to mention the frustration and anger you begin to feel as a result of someone else's thoughtlessness!

To be honest, it is not fair for you and definitely not fair on the clients that follow as they have had the courtesy and respect to get to you on time and yet because of the 'late' client they are now behind schedule in their day as well.

This actually looks bad for you as a business and does not work in your favour when it comes to salon reputation so it is definitely an issue that needs to be addressed and solved in the easiest and best way possible for you and your client.

In this chapter we will be exploring how it affects your salon and the flow of your business and give you some solutions to the problem.

Yes, there are ways to prevent this happening on a regular basis.

Whether your salon is busy or you are still building your clientele up, there will no doubt be clients that are late but there are ways of dealing with a lateness issue that can keep the momentum going for you in your salon.

What would some of the possible reasons be as to why these clients are always late?

Believe it or not, some of them live that way and they honestly do not realise they disrupt others. Actually they may realise, but not think twice about how it affects your salon flow. They are notoriously late for all appointments and events in their life from collecting their children to getting ready for a night out. It becomes part of their nature to be late.

Understanding why a person has a certain 'lateness' habit doesn't excuse it but it does assist you in just accepting them the way they are and making sure their habit does not interfere with the daily running of your salon business.

Naturally there are instances where it cannot be helped and I am sure in most cases the client will be very apologetic and will probably call to let you know and reschedule if necessary. This happens to all of us at one time or another and has to be accepted as a part of your business. Delays in traffic, children becoming suddenly ill, accidents and so on will happen so preventing these late client issues cannot be achieved however you will feel totally different with this situation than you would when someone is late for no other reason except they are late for everything.

As we will discuss in further chapters also, a lot of different situations in your salon will play out differently when a certain level of confidence is reached by you.

Most situations have the same end answer:

Have confidence in yourself, your skills and most of all have respect for yourself and you will find others will follow.

By working on your skills and self confidence, you will be more able to accept people for who they are and where they are in their lives. This does not mean you have to let it disrupt you though ☺

An open heart goes a long way towards personal freedom and empowerment.

Why Are Your Clients Late For Appointments?

This is a question that could have many, many answers to it and also many dimensions of answers to it. Naturally I will be unable to cover all possible reasons as each individual person has unique personalities and unique situations that only they really know. I will however give a few possible scenarios that may help you to understand that getting frustrated is futile but taking action to prevent it is possible.

The first obvious one would be disorganisation in the life of the person who is continuously late. Many people have a mind that goes a million miles an hour and find it difficult to focus on one thing at a time therefore nothing seems to get done. This results in a lifestyle that can be very disorganised which then spreads out to all other areas of their lives, including appointments with others.

Then there is the person who is trying to cram too many things in one day that they can cope with. Whether it is because they are trying to be superwoman/man and be all things to everybody or whether they have just taken on too much to cope with. I know a lot of people like this and it seems more people are heading this way through the pressures of everyday living and a society in which they have to take on many things to survive.

(Fortunately things are changing and new energies are emerging where people are taking on more important things such as family time and self time.)

Of course there are always unexpected things that happen as well such as work commitments changing, traffic jams, accidents and sometimes just the things that life brings up randomly. We all understand these little hiccups and I'm sure they really don't annoy you much in the salon, not as much as the notoriously, deliberately late client but I will be offering some possible scenarios and solutions in this area also.

As a person who is very rarely late, I cannot truly understand how lateness can become such a big part of someone's life but just because I don't understand it does not mean it is bad or wrong, it is just how someone chooses to live and it happens to be different from my ideal.

"It is important to keep in mind that everyone is different in this world we live in. I think if you can accept people for just the way they are, no judgement, the pain and discomfort of a habit you don't particularly like will fade away. And that is all it is, a habit. It is not the person."

Trish Rock

Being compassionate towards people is a gift that I feel most Nail Technicians, Hair Dressers, Makeup Artists and Beauticians have inbuilt. I don't think we would have gotten into a people business if we didn't like people however there are times when you just *wish* they would be different!

You know exactly what I am talking about right!

In a moment I am going to discuss what it means to your salon when clients are late and how you can prevent it from happening but I want you to also understand that if you can accept people who are always late, just as they are, a lot of your frustrations will ease or disappear altogether.

That is just who they are and what they do and you cannot change that.

<u>This does not mean you have to put up with it in your salon</u> but it will assist you on not taking on the frustration and bad feelings associated with getting caught up in the annoyance of it all.

Only the person themselves can change their actions so what is the point of you getting upset, annoyed or frustrated by what they do? You are only hurting yourself by letting it upset and affect you and causing 'dis – ease' in your body and mind. The person you are frustrated with doesn't even know, and most likely doesn't even care, that you are feeling this way!

Let go of the control, accept everyone the way they are and see how much lighter you begin to feel ☺

Preventing Late Clients Affecting Your Salon

It will affect your daily salon schedule when someone is late. There is no doubt at all about that. Not only will it cause disruption to your appointment timings but will also disrupt the clients that are following throughout the day. Many times this will cause chaos especially at really busy times when you are back to back with appointments with no room for error.

There are a few ways to tackle this problem and it will depend on you as to how you go about it. We all run our businesses differently and have different standards and expectations so what I offer here are simply suggestions that may help you to overcome some of the challenges with late clients in a way that will benefit you, your health and your salon.

The first thing is to determine if their lateness is affecting you and your salon in a big way or just in an 'inconvenient' way. There is a difference, albeit a slight one in many cases, but still a difference.

By this I mean is the client more than 10 minutes late? Personally over the years I have had many clients that are always 5 – 10 minutes late and no matter how I tried, what I said or did they would still be late by that small amount of time. It didn't really bother me after a while and as soon as I stopped worrying about it and let it go it didn't affect me physically or mentally.

It really isn't a big deal when you honestly think about it and there are ways to make sure your time, even 5 minutes of it, are not wasted.

Here are some things I suggest you could do to counteract this time in limbo while waiting for the client to come:

1. If you know the person is always 5-10 minutes late, book something else in such as a quick service you may offer, to fill the gap.

2. Book them in 15 minutes later than the time you tell them.

3. If you have to, do their nails, hair or treatment quicker to avoid being late for your next client

4. Enjoy the 10 minute break and have a coffee or something to eat.

5. When I was a smoker it was a perfect time for a quick break.

6. 10 minutes is perfect for fixing one of your own nails, redoing your hair or fixing your makeup.

7. A walk -in client for a quick service can always be slotted in.

8. Restroom break?

9. Pat and cuddle your dog (if you work from home)

10. 5 minutes to check emails or facebook.

You see it doesn't have to be stressful at all. In fact, if you take steps like this you will probably be looking forward to these late clients!

It is a different story of course for the notoriously very late clients!

Personally I would not tolerate them being accepted as clients but that is a decision for you to make yourself, just as are the above suggestions because you may be the person who won't tolerate 10 minutes late either ☺ and that is perfectly ok.

Whatever suits you and your salon situation and the rules in place.

The client that is always more than 15 minutes late? They need to move on to another salon. This may happen for a client every now and then, for unexpected reasons such as an accident, a traffic jam, a sick child, a break down, etc and I think it is safe to say you would accept that and just do your best to get their nails done or rebook a time that is convenient for both of you.

However the person who is constantly this late is a total disruption to your whole salon, staff and other clients and cannot be ignored.

This is how I would deal with this situation:

1. When it happens the first time, let the client know that because they are so late that you can only do a certain amount in the time you have.

2. If they don't like that then they would be advised to rebook and be on time.

3. If they rebook and are late again (very late) tell them the same as you did the first time and either do what you can or rebook.

4. If it happens again, I would cease to rebook them either by telling them directly that you cannot have them as a client or by being conveniently very, very busy for the next few months or more ☺

Here are another 3 scenarios that happen quite often:

1. *The client is late and comes up with an excuse as to the reason and then attempts to make you feel sorry for them. You don't feel sorry and then they attempt to make you feel guilty for not feeling sorry for them.*

You know we all have a choice in life.

If we choose at the last minute to crack under pressure from one of our children to drive them somewhere which in turn leaves us late for an appointment, which was a choice.

If we as the salon owner choose to blame the client that was late for making the rest of the clients late the whole day, then that is a choice we make too.

There is no blame, no excuses. If a client is late, they have chosen that. If you are late because of a late client, then you have chosen that too.

Be strong on your resolve in this and make the choice that is best for you and your other clients that are not late.

2. *Your salon is so busy that to rebook they would have to wait over 4 weeks or wait for a cancellation. In this example you can quite often solve the problem easily either by losing the client or by the client never being late again. A win either way.*

Firing a client can be difficult for some of us. I know for me it was also extremely difficult as I don't like confrontations (nearly as challenging as firing a staff member) The above option is an easier way around it but if you are a strong person you would probably not need to take this exit. You would just tell them ☺

3. *Your salon is not that busy yet and you really need clients so you don't worry if the client is late and do their service anyway.*

This is a confidence and respect issue and if this is the case in your salon may I suggest that it will be far better for you in the long term to adopt the attitude of having a busy salon (just pretend in your mind it is busy and make your decisions from that place).

If you let your very, very late clients get away with this disrespect of you and your services and business they will continue to do so. This will lead to even more lack of confidence for you. It is a vicious cycle that really needs to be stopped before it gets started.

Speak and act as if your salon was extremely busy already. The clients don't know the difference as you don't show them your bookings page and it will allow them to see your value and in turn value your time and work.

You cannot prevent people from having a late habit- you can prevent their habit from affecting your salon.

Nail design by Cheryl Atkins

These ways of dealing with a late client will assist you in running a professional business. If it so happens that you lose a client or two in the process, although I don't like to see that happen, I feel that in some cases it is for the best.

In my experience I have found that most of the clients have valued my time and service enough to make a huge effort to change their lateness. It is often the way you approach them and speak to them that will determine the outcome.

If they know they are a valued client and you want the opportunity to give them the best service possible, and that you need the whole allotted time to do that, they will more likely than not start to arrive on time, or closer to the time anyway!

With practice you will have the confidence to tackle this challenge easily and therein lies the whole solution to any disruptions in your salon.

Confidence to run your business the way you want it to be without others coming in and demanding you do things differently.

I have seen this happen over and over again with students and in fact it still happens every now and then with seasoned professionals but there is a common thread in all cases- lack of confidence in themselves, their work and their business abilities.

It can be a very scary prospect to confront a client about an issue.

How will they react?

What will they say?

Will they come back to the salon?

How will you feel afterwards?

I think the biggest question to ask is:

'How is it affecting you NOW?'

Chances are that the answer to that is not so well, so any reaction from the client will actually be good. If they get upset and leave the salon never to return- great!

If they decide your time needs to be respected and never arrive late again- great!

If you speak to them with kindness, from the heart, and really explain to them why being late affects the whole salon, they will not feel attacked and threatened and will be more likely to listen and respect you.

By honouring yourself and knowing you are worthy of respect by everyone including your clients, you will receive it easily. This will lead to a more flowing salon where every hour will count towards earning income for you.

Remember, this industry is a 'time for money' exchange and your time matters. Sitting in the salon with no clients is not going to provide for your family and pay the bills.

Every hour and every client is important and if you can have a salon full of wonderful, ideal clients that show up on time to every appointment, your days will flow so much more smoothly and effortlessly and you will love being at the salon every day.

This will all begin with your own feelings towards yourself. Know that your time is valuable and you may find that many of the clients you now have that are sometimes late will start arriving on time, the notoriously late clients will disappear and your days will become less frustrating.

Its all a matter of manifesting the exact situation you would like. It starts with knowing how you want to be treated and then believing it can be that way. You must also believe you deserve it...which you DO of course.

So please, talk with those clients that are causing your anxiety and let them know they are a valued customer but could they please help you out by arriving on time more often?

If every now and then you DO still have a client who is late on a continual basis, then perhaps you need to sack them (yes! You can do this).

Also, if every now and then you DO have a moment in the day when a client is a little late, take it as a great sign from the Universe that you needed a breather. And then breathe.

Remember, take each moment for what it is. Bless it. Let it go and enjoy whatever it is anyway!

There are Divine moments each day. Experience them.

Chapter 2

The Loud, Know It All Client

As I look at my appointments for tomorrow I see Miss P is due in.

I wonder what she has done to her nails since her last appointment. Always complaining to me that I do her middle finger crooked! I hate how she grabs the file from me during the appointment and says she can do it better. If she can do them better why is she here bothering me!

And there will be no point letting her know about the fabulous plans I have for my daughter's birthday party as no doubt she will just go on about how I should be doing it and how when she did the same thing it was so much better blah blah blah...

Sound at all familiar to you?

I am sure that every Nail Technician, Beautician and Hair Dresser, no matter how long they have been in the business, has had one of these clients. I am certainly not saying they are bad people, quite the contrary in many cases however it can be a very long appointment hour sometimes right!

Clients like this don't really disrupt your schedule or hold up other appointments however they can really drain you of confidence and energy. A few of them in a row is a killer!

I can honestly say that after 30 years in the Industry, it was only at the very end of my career that I learnt to deal well with this type of client.

> I used to *allow* the discussion of how they knew better than me how to do the nails.

> I used to *allow* them to drain me of all my energy and I used to get very resentful at the end of their appointment that I was now in a bad mood because of them.

These days I know better and my wish for you is to know better too!

"My energy and mood is my decision and choice and if I want to stay in a great frame of mind it will depend on my reactions to people and what they do and say, not the people and what they do or say".

Trish Rock

In this chapter, discussing the loud, know it all client, I want to impress on you that you do not have to have the same feelings that I once experienced. There are many reasons behind the loudness and overtaking attitude and you will discover a new way to see these clients and perhaps even be excited to have them come for an appointment.

Even though they don't disrupt the workings of your daily schedule there is a noticeable difference in the salon atmosphere very often after one of these clients has left.

There are ways to avoid this and some methods may even settle this client a little to be calmer.

You're learning a lesson again from this client and we will take a look at that too at the end of the book.

Personally I could never see any benefit to having clients come in that drained me of all my energy but I now know they too can teach me very special lessons in life.

On the whole, most of the clients that do choose to be loud and very, let's say 'instructional'☺, are really interesting and amazing people too. It just makes it very difficult to get beyond the initial outpouring of advice and knowledge they just *have* to pass on to you when they are so loud and push themselves onto you in a way you just want to block out.

Remain calm my friend, breathe... then take control back. Change the topic, ask them something personal, get them talking about something they love, calm THEM down and enjoy the appointment.

Obviously if you know your ideal client profile and do your marketing based around that, you will have very few of these clients however there will always be the occasion when a loud, obnoxious know-it-all client will come your way and drain you of all you energy and enthusiasm. Learn the steps to overcome that and they will never be a problem to you again.

Understanding why a person can be a little overbearing and loud goes a long way to dealing with the situation in your salon on a daily basis.

Why Are They Loud, Overbearing And Think They Know It All?

Many people make up this world of ours and they all have different personalities. I would estimate that I have dealt with thousands and thousands of clients in my career so far and I have to admit that people can still surprise me.

There are different factors to consider when asking why someone does what they do and in the end it will just boil down to the fact that we are all the result of our past thinking and actions.

Our circumstances will also be an influence on the way we behave and think and I am a strong believer that star signs, numerology, first names and Chinese horoscopes all influence the personality. For instance I have seen over and over again, the person with the same name exhibit the same tendencies and traits. Similar for people born in the same year. I am certain if you have been in the Industry for a while now you will have experienced the same conclusions.

When taking new client details I always enjoy knowing what month a person was born and what year they were born in as I can establish some of the traits I may expect from them. Actually I remember star signs more than names in some instances and my clients would always feel special as I would always know when their birthday was coming up without even looking at my data.

Now having said that, it is not set in concrete and there are always exceptions to the rule but if you deal with the public and are reading this, I'm sure you will agree, in part anyway ☺

So let's get on to some other possible reasons that some people like to be loud and overbearing.

There are times in our lives that we feel unheard. I believe that is true for all of us and mostly starts from childhood. For those of us that are fortunate to be in an environment that is willing to hear us unconditionally, this may not end up being a possible explanation however even if the home environment is great, there is also the school, work and public environment for us all to contend with.

Is it so surprising then that we feel unheard sometimes in this busy society of ours?

And then there are those that experience living in a relationship and household where they are there for everyone else and it seems no one is there to support them. This is a role that we as women often take on. The nurturer, the organiser, the carer, the partner, the parent, the taxi...you get the picture. It is only when it gets to the extreme that we can sometimes get out of touch with ourselves and allow others to control what we do.

Over my years as a Nail tech I have observed that many of the 'know-it-all' clients that I have had and many of the loud overbearing clients have all been in situations where they are not heard fully at home. Now this will not be true for all and I can only express my opinion and knowledge of the clients that have crossed my path.

I know myself during certain times of my life I got a bit loud and tried to take over every conversation and control every situation. Mostly it was because I wanted to be valued and I liked the attention but I have since realised that there are more healthy ways to be valued by others and to get as much attention as needed (although I have to say that once you value yourself, you don't really need others to justify that value or give you attention so much)

If you just accept the client for who she/he is and genuinely listen to what they are saying, usually what will happen is that once you can establish some trust between the two of you, they will settle down and will surprise you with their warmth, care and most of all their story.

When I say 'listen' to the client what I mean is not to listen to their bossiness or instructions on *how to do* your job, but really listen to what they are NOT saying.

> ➢ Do they just want to be taken seriously for a change by someone?

> ➢ Do they want to be heard if only for an hour?

> ➢ Do they need to feel important and valued as a person?

> ➢ Do they want to be recognised as a person, an individual, not a mother, wife, taxi, food provider, cook, cleaner etc?

People just want to be heard in this world. We all want to be respected, heard and valued so if you can do that from the start you will find many of the really overbearing clients will end up being your best clients, long term.

I have found that fear and insecurity will also lead to loudness and control. When people are not secure about themselves and perhaps a little fearful they do not fit in, know what to say or feel awkward in a situation they will just speak over the top of everyone. Of course that goes the other way too and a person can become super quiet and shy.

Whatever the reasons, your clients are not what they appear at first in most cases so give them a chance to speak, make them comfortable and let them know they are welcome in your salon as an individual and that they are valued that way. I am sure after a while you will find they settle down and will love coming to see you because you actually listen to them and treat them with respect and care.

Of course there will still be the ones who continue to tell you how to do your job!

This can be so frustrating and a challenge for us, especially when we are just starting out. You HAVE to be strong. Even if you are not as confident as you could be in the beginning, do not let the clients tell you what to do or not do. Thank them for their input and then CHANGE THE SUBJECT and get on with YOUR work while they are talking.

My suggestion?

Give them the acrylic or gel brush, the supplies to go with it, or the wax, or the scissors, then kick back and get comfortable and tell them to go for it!

Too drastic?

Ok, change the subject:

Agree with them, nod, mumble and generally just say yep, ok and then change the subject.

> Ask them about themselves.
> Ask them something personal.
> Tell them how nice they look.
> Comment on their dress.
> Do anything to get the focus on them and away from the nails.

This of course will all be a confidence issue with yourself.

If you allow them to dictate to you how to do your job, they will continue to do it each appointment.

If you are new to the salon industry it can be difficult but remember this:

✓ You have done the training not them,

✓ You have had the education not them and

✓ You are the one putting the hours of practise in not them.

Nip it in the bud at the first appointment and they will ease off from then on to allow you to do what you need to do.

➢ If they are really persistent about the shape or look of one nail just tell them you will fix it in the next process and move on to the next nail you are doing.

➢ If they are worried about the length, shape or general look of their nails just let them know that at the end you will look at all that and get them all looking perfect for them.

➢ If they think the fringe is not right let them know you will check it again after you dry their hair

➢ If they are worried about what you are doing to their eyebrows or lashes (remember many people have had bad experiences and are frightened) and they want to assist you on the shape, let them know you will be giving them a mirror and they can see the result every step of the way.

And that is what you then need to do- at the end of the process before you paint, gel top coat or finish off the nails, after you have dried the hair off, when the beauty work is nearly finished, ask them if the final result is ok etc and then just spend a few minutes tidying up whatever they ask.

If you can do it all at the end it will not hold up the appointment for too long and you can stick with your timing for the rest of the day.

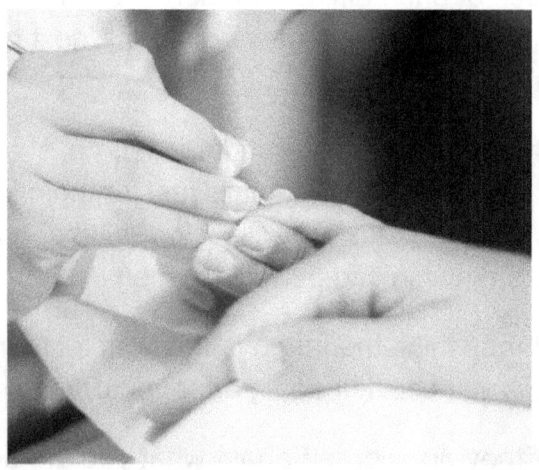

The message overall here is that by accepting each person for who they are and giving them respect, letting them know you value their presence and allowing them to be themselves at their appointment, you may find that the loudness and know-it-all attitudes and behaviours disappear or lesson.

A loyal, interesting and long term client may emerge that you will be pleased about seeing each appointment. It could also go the other way and you could lose the client. Either way it will be good for your salon.

How It Affects Your Salon

Clients that are loud and obnoxious can be a very real disruption to your salon and the other people who are there for their appointments at the same time.

> ➢ If you run a salon from home and are a sole operator, this type of client can really drop the energy in your space and leave you feeling totally depleted when they have gone.

It took many years for me to finally do something about this challenge but eventually I understood that I could control, to a certain extent, the atmosphere in my own salon and could also control my energy and if I chose to give it to others or not.

> ➢ If you are in a salon with other staff members, this type of client can disrupt the whole salon. Remember that other clients may be there for an hour of peace from their busy, 'loud' lives

and don't want someone taking over their relaxation time.

➢ If you rent a space at a nail, beauty or hair salon, a client like this could actually do your business harm as the potential clients in the salon may be turned off from coming to you for a service.

So once I ceased being a victim to it, I discovered there were ways to counteract the clients that would come and zap the energy:

1. **Set the atmosphere in the salon to be calming, relaxing, positive and flowing through the use of crystals, essential oils, music and the placement of furniture (Feng Shui).**

These elements will all help with the flow of energy and the way not only you feel in the salon but how others will feel. An immediate sense of calm as someone walks through the door for their appointment sets the tone for the whole appointment time.

Relaxing and calming elements in your environment can be achieved no matter where your salon is located although often it is difficult to have the music of your choice in some areas.

Crystals such as Rose Quartz and Amethyst will promote love and peace and will dispel negative energy in your salon space. Personally I have a larger one (Amethyst) in the decor somewhere such as the waiting area, the prominent product or display shelf or at the entrance. I then have smaller ones placed nearer to me such as very small ones in a bowl near my table or a smaller one right near me on the desk.

Essential Oils fill the salon air with beautiful scent that can be relaxing and therapeutic at the same time. Look into it a little and select the oils that serve your particular purpose. There are so many available now that you really can pick and choose an exact combination for the desired atmosphere you want to achieve on any one day.

If you are a booth renter and the salon owner does not agree with essential oils being in a burner, you can quite easily place a few drops on the table towels rather than burning them.

I love it when you can smell a salon from outside in the street before you have even gone inside! It makes me want to go in. The atmosphere is already set to be calm and relaxing and you will attract relaxing clients.

Of course be careful not to make the smell overpowering as this will cause problems such as allergies and unpleasant reactions, feeling uncomfortable while in the salon and also not everyone likes the same scents.

Be subtle, use a pleasant aroma and make it a pleasure for all who come to your salon that day, as well as yourself and staff.

Furniture placement can be just as important in your salon for energy flow. Following the practice of Feng Shui, allowing an energy flow around and among your furniture pieces will really help with a better salon atmosphere.

Have you ever sat somewhere in a room and felt tired? Yet you could sit elsewhere in that same room and feel invigorated? This is the energy flow and there are many great books out there as well as many resources online to investigate the best way for you salon to be positioned.

2. Protect yourself from the energy takers

It is simple to put up an invisible force around you to prevent others from 'stealing' your energy. With practise this can be done easily.

Imagine there is a glowing bright light that surrounds your whole body. Now imagine that as you are with another person this bright light is being shared and experienced by you and the other person. This happens every time we are near others. Energy is always exchanging from us and to us.

Often times however there are clients that want to suck more out of you to replenish their own energy. The way to prevent this and to not feel depleted at the end of an appointment is to just imagine you have a shield around you that is protecting your light.

Don't allow your energy to be taken.

At the times when it is really becoming challenging, think about something great that this client has or does. A really wonderful quality they may have. Your mind can wander off to a better place and your energy will be in tact with these better thoughts of the person.

If you do allow your energy to be zapped, you will gradually feel more and more tired for the rest of the day, you will feel uninspired and you will feel resentful and angry at life and everyone in it. Often this is then carried back to the family who actually had nothing to do with it but are the ones who end up with YOUR bad energy and mood.

This was certainly one of my biggest discoveries and lessons in the final years of working in a salon and it is a skill I take with me wherever I am and no matter what business I am doing as I will always be dealing with people, and there will always be energy takers.

3. Remain calm

Remaining peaceful and keeping your client at ease will make a big difference. As discussed before, start to ask you client some personal questions so they can talk about themselves. (a disclaimer here: please be careful about what you actually ask people as some are not willing to share and will be offended by your asking.)

Best to start off with asking where they got their top, earrings etc or what they think of their new car or something on that level to get the ball rolling and see what they are prepared to share with you.

The whole thing here is to get them to quieten down and stop bossing you around!

Asking them about themselves or complimenting them on their clothes, hair, jewellery or anything you can find that seems as though they would get a lift from you asking, will change the energy and the conversation.

It doesn't always work but it certainly wiorth trying and as a salon owner I would know this about you: you can, and do, do this easily.

I have found in my experience that as soon as you refuse to allow clients to come and take over, claim your energy and show you how to do your work, that many will become wonderful long term clients that refer others.

On the other hand there are also those who decide to go elsewhere. They go to someone else who WILL allow it. So I say good riddance and good luck. More room for a better client to come ☺

Remember life is a choice and you can choose what you give out and to whom.

Its...

- ✓ YOUR salon

- ✓ YOUR hard work

- ✓ YOUR rules

All the while still giving absolutely fantastic customer service and treatment second to none.

Chapter 3

The Constant 'No Show' Client

It's now 2.30pm and Miss M hasnt shown again! This is getting beyond a joke!

Another lost hour of income and a spot that someone on my cancellation list, someone who respects my time and values her appointment, could have had.

What is it with these people? If they are not going to come for their appointment why do they make one in the first place? They seem to have no respect for me, my salon or the other loyal clients that do get here on time because they really want their nails done!

The client that constantly just does not show up can be a salon breaker.

I believe every business has these clients and every business deals with them in a different way but the feeling about them is the same:

Why do they do it and how can the situation be turned around.

Some of the same personality traits are present here with this type of client as they are for the client who is constantly late, although I would rather have a slightly late client than a no show!

Disrupting others doesn't seem to be an issue to them and in fact many of them would even be unaware that their actions are affecting others. They are so caught up in their own world, they are totally blind to the fact that not showing for an appointment can lead to distress for another person.

It is even more challenging to think that you could ever like this type of client but there have been occasions in my salons where the tables have turned and the client that had previously had a few no shows, became more aware of everyone's time and always showed for appointments after that.

Once again, in this case it is up to you as to how you react and what the outcome is.

*"Getting frustrated at certain situations is part of life but to **remain** that way is your choice. You can choose to stay in that frustration or feel a better emotion instead. The choice is yours." Trish Rock*

There are ways to deal with the clients that just don't show up with no call, no notice and certainly no apology that we will explore in this chapter. I also wish to give you some possible life situations that may be affecting your clients that will in turn bring them to the state of unawareness in their actions.

This busy society of ours certainly affects a lot of people but even closer to home people lives are extremely busy and filled with extra family duties and responsibilities these days so is it any wonder that an appointment can be forgotten?

I feel to really put a stop to this habit that some clients are notorious at, it has to be understood a little more.

Believe me I was not in a mindset to understand these people a few years back but now I can display more compassion towards them as I can see beyond the exterior of their actions and can see that behind all of it that often there are bigger issues at play.

It is just unfortunate that your salon is the one that cops the empty appointment every so often and believe me you are not the only business person experiencing this!

So as we discover why someone does not show up to appointments and how they may have come to that state of mind, you may also see that you can think and react differently to the situation.

I will also give you some solutions in your salon for avoiding this type of client and ensuring that all of your clients show up for their appointments, on time, giving you a more flowing salon with far better success and results.

Why Would A Client Make An Appointment And Then Not Show Up?

This is an interesting question and one that is fun to explore although we will never really know the definitive answer to it as each individual is different and each situation is different.

The first situation would be that something happened to a client on the way to you and they just could not get there. In most of these instances the client would call and let you know, therefore giving you time to call a client from your waiting list, take a walk in client or send out a quick *Push Notification* through your Salon App to fill the spot. (For information on an App specially designed for your salon contact me at trish@strategicbusinessapps.com or check out http://strategicbusinessapps.com or my facebook page at http://facebook.com/strategicbusinessapps)

Very rarely have I found that clients who are unable to make it due to a random occurrence will forget to call you and let you know. They will then make another appointment.

The next examples are my own experience of clients in my salons that have displayed this behaviour. They are only *my thoughts* on the matter but may just offer you some food for thought when you are beginning to feel frustrated and angry at these clients.

It is easy to get upset and angry too because after all we have a business to run!

One of the clients that did this at my salon actually had some serious control problems happening at her home. She had allowed the situation to become quite bad and to the detriment of her own wants, needs and respect. She was under strict 'control' of every move she made by her partner, a situation that I don't understand fully but one that happens to many people and is not obvious.

She wasn't 'allowed' to have her nails done and yet she continued to make appointments. I am guessing it made her feel better when she made the appointment, as if she had control of her life just for a moment. It happened about once every few months and I always hoped that when she booked that *this* would be the time she came. *This* would be the time she said no to the control and did something for herself. Unfortunately it only ever happened once, she was thrilled with her nails but I could see she was very concerned about whether she would keep them for long or not.

At the time of course I thought she was very weak not being able to stand up to the partner however these days I have come to understand that there are more reasons than I could ever, or will ever, see behind what this lady did and who she was.

I have a lot more compassion and understanding about her now and others in the same position and although I still don't fully understand it, I know it is not my concern.

It is a concern in regards to the **smooth operation** of your salon however and if you can honestly see that a client is never going to respect that fact that you are running a business and you rely on them to honour the appointment they have made with you, then it would be best to let them go and find a client that will.

Au revoir

There was another instance of a client that booked and didn't show up quite regularly in my salon. She was a very nice lady with a great personality and mostly happy whenever I was having a conversation with her.

This particular lady was a happy go lucky person however she was the type of person who had never worked with people before, had never had any working experience with jobs that involved appointments and did not understand why people would get upset when she did not show.

I feel these clients are possibly the worst as they usually come with an attitude as well, or the total opposite- total vagueness about the whole thing!

Surely you would agree that because we work by appointments daily, we have a greater respect and understanding for any business we have to book in to see? There would be very few circumstances that if I could not make it to the appointment that I would not call and let them know, one of them being if I was in an accident or something serious like that of course which I would not wish upon anyone.

People who do not understand this do not respect it and therefore do not respect your time and business either. While I now have compassion for these types of people too, you really don't want them in your salon if you can help it.

That may sound harsh to some but let's be honest, you are running a professional business and you need to have your booking spots filled with people who respect your time, work and salon.

If you cannot help this client see that your time is valuable, then you may be better off with a client who does.

I find that a lot of the public think that we just sit around all day and play with glitter and nail polish, muck around with our hair and play with makeup.

The profession of doing nails, hair and beauty is often not taken seriously by people so it is up to us, as business owners, to keep this in mind and make sure we are always behaving and speaking like the serious professionals we are. This will go a long way to attracting clients that value your time and skills and also know and respect the fact you are running a business that supports you.

In a moment I will give you some solutions to stop or prevent no shows but first I just want to say that even though we can get very annoyed and disrupted by these clients, there may be circumstances in their lives that we either don't understand, don't agree with or don't know.

Whatever the case may be it is not for us to judge. We just need to be understanding and compassionate towards them and as I have said before, accept people for who they are.

That does not mean however that you have to let it affect your business.

How To Avoid The 'No Show' Client Affecting Your Salon

There are a few different things you can implement in your salon to prevent this type of client disrupting the daily routine and leaving you with empty appointment spots where you do not earn income.

Your livelihood is dependent on your bookings being filled and if your salon is busy, you will have a waiting list of very keen, great clients that would love to get an appointment with you. When you have a no show it can be such a waste of a booking for you, and frustrating as well.

If your salon is not that busy yet, allowing no shows to keep letting you down will only encourage them to keep doing it.

It all comes down to a respect- for you, your salon and mostly your time, which actually starts with **you** respecting yourself and your time first.

After all, if you do not respect what you do why would your clients?

> ➢ The first thing you can implement into your salon is a rule that if a client does not show for an appointment that they are still liable for the cost of that appointment.

I would suggest placing a sign somewhere in your salon stating this. I would also send out a broadcast to your clients via email or letter and I would also suggest placing this notice on your Facebook, Twitter, LinkedIn and Website pages.

The wording could be as follows:

Please note that when making an appointment with this salon that you agree to paying, in full, the cost of the appointment if you do not show for that time.

Or

When making a booking with our salon please be aware that if you do not show for your appointment it is our policy that you will still be required to pay for that appointment.

This policy works for many salons and has cut the amount of no show clients down considerably and in many cases has stopped them entirely.

Introducing this into your salon may take a lot of self confidence but be brave my friend, remember that this is your business, this is your dream and this is the way you earn your living. Having all of your clients show up is important as you need the income from each and every hour that you are operating.

> ➢ The next thing I would suggest to you would be to use your common sense with these clients. If you can see that they will become, or already are, a problem to your salon, think carefully about whether you really want them as clients.

Do you really want this stress every few weeks?

Do you have other clients that would really value your time more?

If you are still building your clientele, are these the type of clients you really want?

Maybe you can see past the issues that they may be having at home or work or personally and will give them a few more chances. That works in some cases and they will become very loyal, terrific clients.

If not, either tell them you are not prepared to have them at your salon, and the reasons why. Or simply just be busy whenever they call for an appointment ☺

> ➢ A routine of calling or sending sms to clients who are booked in is essential to running a serious nail business. Make it a rule to go through and make sure all appointments have been reminded the day before. This reduces a lot, if not all, of lateness and no shows.

Many operational systems in salons now will have this done automatically each day and some salons will have a nominated person to do the task. Either way, if you make the time to do this activity your salon will run a lot more smoothly.

I know myself I love when I get an sms or a quick reminder call about an appointment I may have that week or the next day. I believe it shows professionalism and care in the salon.

In some cases it also gives an apprentice an activity that builds confidence and customer service skills so not only are you making sure your clients are all coming for their appointment but you are training your staff at the same time.

It is so important to remember that you are in a service industry. This means that you make money per person as opposed to per product where you can be selling to many people at once.

Your Time ➡️ Your Income

If you are not utilising your time, and the time of your staff members, it will be lost income.

Earning a reasonable income to support your family and lifestyle is not a difficult achievement in the salon industry. Earning an income that exceeds the average requires you to be vigilant with your business practices and think bigger.

Getting your clients to all arrive on time and regularly for their appointments is one thing that you can have greater control over just by putting systems in place in your salon on a daily basis.

There are also many different types of online booing systems that can be utilised to ensure that when people book in with you- it is paid for immediately. This means that if they don't show- they lose their money. I know this system is working brilliantly in many salons.

Of course when you set this up you may have a lot of fears running through your head such as whether people will book with you or not with such strict conditions. Believe me, they will. It is being proven again and again by salons worldwide who have these booking systems in place.

Your salon does not have to be the same as the others around you. In fact, it would be better for your salon if you were different! Make the choice to be different. Decide to not let no-show clients take over your emotions and affect salon income.

Attract clients that value your time and the challenges will be less, income will be more and your success will be easier to achieve.

"Often we lack the courage to pursue what we dream of in our life for fear others will laugh at us, squash our ideas and tell us to get real. They are usually the ones who didn't get to pursue their dreams so in fact you would be doing them a great service by reaching your dream as that will then give them a shining light to follow in the pursuit of their own happiness."

Trish Rock

Chapter 4

The Hypochondriac

'How are you Miss G?'

"Oh...I'm ookkaaayy...if only this headache would disappear and I could get some sleep.

The doctor said I had to start taking this medication to help me with my stress and it has given me nothing but problems and the pain of this headache will not go away and now my eyes are sore because I cant sleep and I'm even more stressed!

My mother used to have headaches like this so it is no wonder I have it too. I think I also have the bad knee she suffered from and may have to have it operated on soon because it is giving me a lot of pain and I cant bend it much........"

I feel a headache coming on just thinking about this troublesome client!☺

Seriously though we have all had them, still have them or will be getting them into our salons. Mostly they are very lovely people but they can be so, so draining after an hour.

I don't believe this type of client affects the salon as much as they affect *you* and *your energy* while you are talking to them during the appointment.

In my experience, I have not had too many of these clients on a regular basis but there was one, that I will tell you about soon, that really gave me the opportunity to see things a different way and act differently when she was at her appointment.

There are many reasons why someone acts like this and some of them may be genuine!

It used to really drain me when I had a hypochondriac client in. I guess I had a bit of history in that area too with my mother deteriorating over the years and having many complaints and ailments- some real- some imaginary.

I just didn't, and still don't, understand why someone would choose to be sick and not want to get better.

This type of client may not affect you at all.

Perhaps you **enjoy** giving them sympathy and finding out about all of their ailments, what has been done, what can be done, all the different treatments they have had, hearing their history of illness each appointment and generally giving them the 'You poor thing!' response which is what they want.

If that is the case, maybe you should skip this chapter. Its not a good or bad thing. There is no wrong or right.

I was like that in the beginning of my career but after a few years, and definitely after 30 years, you really just don't want to hear it anymore. That may be a little too harsh and honest for some to hear but it's the truth for me.

Personally, I found that sickness just wasn't, and still isn't, part of my life. I am fortunate enough to experience well being and just think that everyone should. Well that's how I used to think anyway.

These days I know better and I understand that there is a reason why people act as they do - Reasons that are very real and important to the person but that you and I may never know or comprehend, or even wish to explore.

Why have I included this type of client into this book?

I believe that even though they are not affecting your salon so much, they really do drain you of your energy if you allow it and I want to have a look at how you can prevent that and understand this person a little better.

I may appear a little hardened in this section of the book. This is just my personality and life experiences showing up I guess and if you ask my family they will agree- I don't like false health complaints and whinging. There was a rule in our house when the kids were growing up – no blood, no sympathy and even now my daughter brings it up and my son reminds me of that and he is nearly 30!

I have matured a little now and have a lot more compassion for people who are not experiencing well being for the most part ☺

If you happen to be attracting many clients like this there may be a reason for that which we will take a look at later at the end of the book but for now I would like to describe an experience I had with a client many years back.

This lady was actually a very nice, kind lady and she came to me on a regular basis for over 3 years.

Things started out ok, just normal I suppose for a new client. We got on well and I enjoyed her company.

Over the years though she became very different and at the end, just before I stopped doing nails, she really was a full on hypochondriac.

(To be honest, she began to 'appear' worse but this had more to do with how I was thinking about life at the time. I have discovered that over that period of time I was becoming very dissatisfied with the way my life was heading and unfortunately I began to blame everyone around me, including clients, but more on that later in the book.)

I think what annoyed me the most was that no matter what the conversation was, it always led back to an ailment she had somewhere in her body. Whatever I attempted to talk about was sliced straight through the middle with a remark and story about the bad knee, the bad back, the way things *just were* because that's how her mother was and that's why she is like it blah blah blah.

Very draining and frustrating, so much so that I began to dread the appointments and actually just hoped she would be no show client!

To make things worse she would do her own nails in between appointments also and by the time she had buffed and buffed and finally got back to me, the nail plates were thin and often red and sore which made my work tricky. To be honest, I didn't feel comfortable sometimes putting anything on the nails but she insisted they were ok and so I went ahead. There were never any other complications or bad results from the nails- just the thinness.

You may be thinking at this point I needed to have taken more confident actions and just not had any empty appointments for her when she wanted to book in! It was difficult to say no after so long as she had been a regular client for over 2 years and although she was draining I still wanted her to have beautiful nails and hands.

This is why I can easily relate to many of the techs who find it a challenge to let these clients go. You know you really need to, for the sake of yourself and energy, but something just stops you from doing it. Weird and confusing at times but a fact none the less.

What is the best way to deal with this in your salon? Well, firstly, this type of client may not bother you at all so if that's the case, great.

If you are being drained by someone similar, here is what to do:

Chill.

Yes, in the end I just realised she had been craving attention her whole life (self esteem issues etc) and this is how she got it. From her husband, her family, the doctors, her workplace. It satisfied her and made her life seem better so really there is nothing anyone can do but to be understanding and compassionate.

Attempting to change her was futile. Attempting to make her see another point of view was futile and even thinking of encouraging her to be well was out of the question.

Towards the end of our nail journey, I just stopped getting worked up about it and actually just ignored most of it. I zoned out to another place and every now and then would ask something positive, try to get a laugh and attempt to change the subject (which rarely worked, I have to say!). The total appointment time was usually only about 30 minutes so it wasn't a huge stretch to get through.

It made no difference to the appointment, no difference to the experience she had at my salon but what it did do was give ME a better experience and stopped draining me of my energy. My frustration then ended. I enjoyed the time more.

Also at that stage I had begun some personal development techniques that were allowing me to see with clearer vision the world around me and the part I had to play in that. So perhaps this is more a story about the changes in me than anything else however there are a lot of occasions in a salon situation where we can be drained of all our good energy and this is certainly one of them.

If you do feel drained at any stage after appointments give yourself a few minutes to shake it off and get your good energy back.

Go to the restroom if you have to but just give yourself a few moments to get away from everyone, to breathe deeply and relax within. It helps.

If you happen to have a very lively client afterwards this will be wonderful to restore your full enthusiasm back and be able to lift the spirits of others again.

Designing your Ideal Client profile really helps to attract the clients you really want into your salon which goes a long way in avoiding the clients that are going to drain you of your energy and enthusiasm.

This is one of the most important areas I see in laying the foundations of your business and the reason I work on it intensely when mentoring my clients now. A face to face business such as nails, hair and beauty will be a lot more enjoyable, and ultimately more successful for you if you can attract the clients that suit you best and whom you really want to deal with.

Chapter 5

The Cheap Client

"Hi, I would like to make an appointment please but could you tell me what discounts or specials you have available at the moment?"

"Good morning, could you tell me the price to have my nails done and if I have them

already filed for you would it be cheaper?"

"I cant believe it costs that much to have my nails done here at your salon, I think I will just go to the other place that has them for half that price and I don't even have to

Have you had conversations like this in your salon?

It can be really frustrating some days when you have a lot of clients that appreciate you and value you and then you have to deal with these clients too, the ones that don't respect your time at all.

Once again I refer back to knowing who your *ideal client* is and attracting them, not the ones you don't want however in the world at the moment there is a lot of concern for where we spend our money and every dollar counts so we cannot criticise the person who wants the best deal, but we can say no to the person who wants quality work done for nothing.

Having others value your time is so important no matter what you do, where you work or what business you are running.

Even more important and essential for the success and longevity of your business is YOUR belief and the value YOU place on yourself and your services.

The quality of your Salon business will be determined by the quality of the clients that is coming in regularly to it.

Discounts and special offers are a part of any business but usually they are in the form of a marketing campaign to get new clients in, a campaign to thank existing clients or a special offer to get a new staff member busy or promote a new product you are introducing to the salon.

I think the thing to remember here is that while you will get the cheap clients taking full advantage of any special offers you decide to have, if you can show them the **value** and service they will expect to receive in your salon and give them the **experience they desire**, they will then **value you** and will continue to come to your salon- at your price point.

Another type of 'cheap' client is the one that goes salon hunting for bargains, or has been having nails done at a lower quality salon for a while and does not know the difference between great nails and a cheap job that looks bad and wont last.

As Nail Techs is it difficult for us to believe sometimes that someone can think their nails look great when in fact they are the worst job ever! I am certain this is true for Hair Dressers and Beauticians also. Unfortunately they are not around nails, hair and beauty as much as we are and often they really don't know the difference.

Client Education is the key here.

The clients that come to you from other salons and need a whole lot of work done to restore the quality of their nails, hair and beauty treatments need:

➢ Firstly, to be shown what great nails, hair or beauty treatments can look like and how they are better for their overall appearance and the health of their nails, hair and skin.

➢ Secondly, to be informed, before the appointment commences, how much time it will involve, what procedure will be required and how much this 'fix up' will cost.

This will come down to the confidence you have in dealing with clients and the respect you have for yourself but I encourage you to try it. It may feel awkward at first but remember this is *your* livelihood and *your* time- *you have control* over it.

If you want to have a Salon business that earns you the income you desire, you need to have clients that are willing and able to pay the price you set. And it is up to you to determine how much income you can earn and up to you to decide what the prices are.

As I said earlier, this is a one on one business so your **time is money**. Determine how many hours you wish to work and how much per hour you need to earn and then you can reasonably come up with the price for your services.

Of course your prices need to be in alignment with the area and the other salons around you but if you have really embraced something unique about your services and are the only one offering what you do and how you do it, then adjust your prices accordingly, to reflect that.

The clients I consult with to improve their salons really begin to see the bigger picture of where their salon could be and where it could take them as soon as they embrace their uniqueness and really market it to their ideal clients.

 It makes so much difference to the quality of your business and makes dealing with your clients a more pleasurable experience, more often and I know you can experience this too just by believing in yourself and your salon.

When you made the decision to open your salon, did you do it just so you could play with nails, hair and makeup all day or did you do it for other reasons such as:

- ✓ To provide a better income and allow a better lifestyle for your family

- ✓ To have the freedom to choose your own hours and work conditions

- ✓ Be your own boss and play by your own rules

I am betting that these are some of the exact reasons you got into business so therefore it stands to reason that you want to be taken seriously in your business and you want to become a more successful business owner correct?

Unless you do just want to 'play' nails all day just for fun as a hobby? Well, that would be ok too but don't expect to make any money from doing it that way.

Getting better clients into your salon is a great start to having the business you desire. Your Ideal Client profile will lead you in the right direction as to who you want in the salon, where they are located, how to find them and the best way to market to them.

By targeting the clients you really want you will eliminate the attraction to the other clients that are not so desirable.

Some of the most interesting and exciting clients I dealt with over the years were the successful business people. I guess because I was determined to have success in my business I wanted to hear what they did and how they did it.

These clients were great teachers and mentors for me which I why I wanted them and attracted them to my salons.

"To be successful you have to be around successful people. They have the answers. They have the encouragement and they will lift you higher than the naysayer."

Trish Rock

You know, the best way to learn business is by networking with others who already are successful at it. So this will mean hanging around other salon owners, networking with other nail techs, hair dressers and beauty professionals and also hanging out with other business owners who will show you and teach you how to play a bigger game. They will show you how to invest and manage your money, they will show you the best way to organise your accounts etc and they will also encourage you and be positive which is something that is not always available in your family environment.

In my experience over the years of networking with other Nail Techs and industry professionals, I believe there are those who are very intimidated by the more 'successful' clients that come to their salons. They view them as being stuck up, too interested in themselves and perhaps even that they think they are better than everyone else.

Usually this type of client will be very affluent and an ideal client to have attracted to your salon not only from the income side of things but also the personal experience.

Learn what you can from all people who come into your life and salon but especially take notes from the successful people because they have already done what you want to do.

Make changes to the way you deal with the 'cheap' clients that come your way and eventually you will either stop attracting them or you will convert them into loyal, lifetime clients who will value your skills and time and refer like crazy!

Why Are Successful Clients Great For Your Salon?

I believe this is the exact person you need to be attracting to your salon. Why? Well there are quite a few reasons, some of which we have mentioned already. Let's have a look now at two of the benefits:

1. Income.

Attracting successful, affluent clients to your salon will give you more income. These clients, while they are usually very wise with their money, will pay for quality and service. They understand how business works. They will never be late or decide to not show up. They value your time and your skills and they respect the fact that you are stepping out and stepping up by deciding to have your own business.

2. Referrals

You will gain a lot of referrals from these clients, more than the cheap clients that are just after a discount. The referrals they send to you will be people who are similar and of course we all know- the more referrals you get the less marketing for clients you have to do! Referrals are the best way to get new business because they are already in love with your salon and services before they even get there. There is no convincing, there is no haggling and there is no doubt in their minds that they are going to get the service and quality they were told about.

It can be a challenge for us to deny a client an appointment in our salon. I totally understand this and can admit to being weakened by it. Seeing the awful work that someone else has done and knowing you can do better, knowing the client will have better looking nails, hair or skin and also knowing they will be healthier nails, hair or skin is sometimes too much of a conscious task to let go of.

Remember this- there are other salons that will do them. Do not worry.

You don't need ALL the clients.

You only need the ones you desire to have and believe me there are plenty of them if you are looking in the right places, with the correct marketing and the right attitude and mindset.

In fact, if you get it right, you don't even have to look for clients because you will simply be attracting them to you- the ones you want- your ideal clients.

Once you get the right message into the marketplace, with your strategies and promotions, and go after the people who you really want in your salons, you will start to see the amazing clients that you desire.

Trust in yourself and your ability.

You have done the training and you have the skills so remember that next time someone wants you to do a quality job but only wants to pay you for the quality of an unskilled tech.

Your time is valuable, your work is worth paying for and your salon is professional, educated and top quality. Demand clients atht will appreciate that about you and your salon.

Believe in yourself, your passion and your vision of a successful salon.

It can be very challenging in the beginning wen you need all the clients you can get, so that you can pay your bills and stay afloat. But once that time has passed, become more choosey. Target your ideal clients. Create a marketing message that will attract the clients that will appreciate your work.

If you require some help in that area, there are 2 books you might also like to read:

The Nail Technicians Guide To Outperforming and Outlasting The Competition.

and

Salon Client Attraction- Attract More Clients, Earn More Profits with the G.L.O.S.S System- 5 Steps to Salon Success.

I am the author of both and they are available from Amazon. They will help you attract the exact clients you want.

Summary

We want to help you regain clarity about your individual power. Everyone has it. No one can ever take it away from you. No one can ever do anything "bad" to you. No one can assert into your experience. Everything, without exception, comes only by your individual invitation to it.

Do you understand the process of asking? When you give something your attention and it becomes your dominant vibration relative to the subject—that is your asking.

So, deliberate creating is not so much about looking out into the world and saying, "Oh, there are things that are good that I want to create or attract into my experience, and there are things that are bad that I don't want to create or attract into my experience."

Deliberate creating is more about deliberate allowing. Deliberate allowing is more like deliberate vibration.

--- Abraham

Being clear on what you want from your life is the first step to creating the life you want. Being clear on who you want to fill your salon business is the first step to having the business you want.

While not all of the clients described may be causing frustrations and challenges for you at the present time, I would hazard a guess that there would be at least one causing some pain and frustration.

One of the biggest messages I have had in recent times is that **we attract what we need to show us the things we want to learn to grow and move forward in our lives.** This is the case whether we know it or not.

You can live unconsciously and not realise that people are sent to you as teachers or you can live consciously and understand that everyone and everything that comes to us is a blessing, a teacher, a lesson and a way to expand into the full life we are here to experience.

How Are These Clients Benefiting Our Own Personal Growth?

For many years I thought that I was living in control of my life when in fact I was being a victim to it. I thought I had worked well with what had been given to me and I made good choices. I believed that everything that happened to me was because of *other* people and that I had nothing to do with that.

So of course I began to build up resentment of other people. I wanted a certain life and *they* were stopping me from getting it! My goodness I must have been such a drain on everyone around me with all my whinging and complaining!

I blamed my misery on relationships that were not giving me what I wanted. I blamed it on my work. I blamed it on my clients and I blamed it on society.

One of the very powerful events that happened at one stage in my life (lets just say- an out of body experience and a story for another book ☺) helped me to understand that there was more. There was more than I was seeing and I needed to get to a place within myself where I could see it clearly.

This is what I desire for you too.

One of the driving forces behind everything I do, including putting pen to paper (fingers to keyboard) for this book, is to show you how you really can *design a life* that you want.

I have learned that everyone who enters our life, and everyone who doesn't, is assisting in our clearer vision of how we can be.

All of the clients I have mentioned in this book are messengers. I can only speak for myself, and what they have taught and shown me, because for you it will be different.

But I can assure you that if you are feeling resistance towards someone or something it is for a reason and you are meant to grow with the teaching.

If we are not experiencing challenges in our lives it will mean we are not moving forward and growing and the same goes with our businesses.

Here are some of the ways that clients have shown me things about myself that I have learnt and grown from- as soon as it became clear to me that this is what was happening of course!

I had to start living consciously and deliberately rather than by default and when I made that shift, everything changed.

- ✓ I began to see that the clients who were constantly late and had a million excuses were showing me that I was in fact in a 'victim' mentality like they were and I had a million excuses about why my life was not going the way I thought it should be going.

✓ I began to see that the 'cheap' clients were showing me that I had a 'poverty' consciousness like they did. And as soon as I shifted that belief and began to hang around and interact with successful people things changed for me financially.

✓ I began to see that the 'hypochondriac' clients were coming to me so that I may learn to be more compassionate with others and as soon as I had that shift, my heart, which had been closed for a long time, began to overflow with love and understanding for others.

✓ I realised that I was the 'loud' person on many occasions and it was because I was not being heard, by myself and others.

We can choose to blame everyone around us for the circumstances we find ourselves in and for the challenges that face us but when we realise that we have created everything in our lives with the way we think about things, big changes can occur.

People we come across in life are reflections of what we want to see about ourselves. This is easily understood and accepted when we are with pleasant people whom we respect and love but the same is also true for the people who challenge us and are persistent in that exercise.

The next time you are faced with a feeling of anger or resentment, annoyance or frustration – think about what it is about this person, what are the things that are *really* annoying you and *where do you see that in your life and manner.*

It is an interesting exercise to do and can be difficult at first, especially if you don't wish to see some of the things about you that may need adjusting but it is an individual experience and one that only you can take. And only if you are ready.

It works at the other end of the scale also in those times when perhaps you are feeling less valued, less important and generally not feeling that good about yourself, have a think about who and what comes into your life on those days? Are you hearing and seeing the messages that are all around you?

"Life will bring us messages, if only we would see them, feel them and hear them. Be still, be silent. Listen for the empty space in between the words and the sounds. There you will find the next step."

Trish Rock

Learning to *love* the clients that you *sometimes just want to hate* is a simple shift in the way you think about those clients and about yourself.

I am in no way saying that you need to put up with destructive or salon breaking behaviour from clients and I would definitely advise you to take some of the steps I have suggested to avoid that.

What I am saying though is that once you shift the way you are thinking, everything changes and you see things in a different way. Who you attract will change and your whole attitude in the salon will become conscious rather than haphazard.

The clients whom you thought to be annoying and frustrating will fade away and you will wonder why they were such a noose around your head for so long. Many of them will simply go elsewhere and there will be some who you see in a totally different way who will become your best clients.

If you are going to have a business where you are face to face with people each day, make sure the people are the ones you want to be face to face with.

Start with exploring your ideal client profile, attracting into your salon those ideal clients and then having an understanding that people are not what they appear to be at first glance (most people anyway!). Go deeper; really listen to what they are saying, and not saying, to fully grasp where they are in their lives and perhaps where some of the behaviour is coming from.

Have confidence in yourself and respect what you do. Others will soon follow.

I trust you have received value in the suggestions given in this book and I wish you a very successful and fruitful business and career.

Let me conclude by saying this:

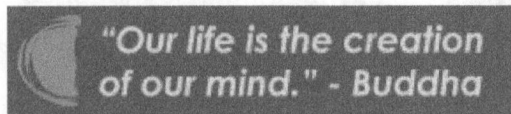
"Our life is the creation of our mind." - Buddha

We are what we think.

What are YOU thinking today?

About the author

Trish is an entrepreneur who has embraced the digital age of communication and relationship building.

In retail business since 1989, and now a successful mobile app developer, Trish says the key to success is the experience you give to your customers.

She has written 2 books that teach this business philosophy as well as a home study course, audio products and a webinar series. She has also contributed to 6 books on business, social media and mindset and writes a regular column on business, marketing and mobile app technology for a global magazine and a national magazine.

Trish has won awards for design excellence as well as outstanding business achievement and growth.

She is a sought after app designer and developer as well as a speaker and media presenter with a following in social media and blogging.

In her Nail career, Trish had numerous successful Salons as well as being an employer, a competition winner, a judge, an educator and also a consultant.

She has established Salon businesses in hairdressing salons, beauty salons, stand alone premises and also at home. She has also had a mobile business.

Nails Magazine featured her Salon Client Attraction (G.L.O.S.S.) Home Study Course, which shows step by step, how to establish the correct foundations of a successful salon.

Working now as an App developer, Trish creates custom Apps for Salons and other businesses. These are marketing tools that are on the leading edge and every business will benefit as the world of mobile marketing opens up.

Find out how you can get started and begin to have:

- ✓ The salon of your dreams
- ✓ The income you desire
- ✓ The clients you want and plenty of them
- ✓ Marketing Strategies that WORK
- ✓ Uniqueness
- ✓ MORE profits
- ✓ MORE loyal clients and
- ✓ MORE of the life you desire

"After nearly 30 years in the Nail Industry, I can honestly say that if this form of marketing had been available when I had my salons, I would have been the first to line up for one!

Your clients are mobile and you need to reach them where they are looking. Simple, easy and time effective, a mobile app not only give you a connection to your customers but stands you out in the marketplace as an innovative and progressive salon business."

Here are some of the advantages of going mobile:

- Instant and free SMS communication to your clients

- Lead Generation

- Referral systems

- Shopping Cart system

- Loyalty programs

- Booking systems

- Easy and fast website browsing

- Social connect

- One tap calling and emailing

- Location maps and more

To find out how you can have your customers browsing, booking and buying more easily, contact Trish to arrange a complimentary call where you can go through some ideas that will bring a great ROI and many other benefits.

Looking For A New Solution To Having Your Customers Connect Easily, Quickly and Effectively?

Looking For A More Flexible Way To Market Directly To Your Audience & Get Bums On Seats?

Contact Trish:

Email: trish@strategicbusinesapps.com

Web: www.strategicbusinessapps.com

Web: www.nailsalonsuccesscoach.com

Facebook: www.facebook.com/strategicbusinessapps

Facebook: www.facebook.com/nailsalonsuccess

Helping Salon Owners With Client Attraction
And Salon Marketing To Increase
Profitability and Longevity.